Get Up and GO!

Get Up

and

GO!

The History of American Road Travel

Sylvia Whitman

Lerner Publications Company • Minneapolis

To Ben and Will Foster, the furriest "vroommates" I know

The following people and organizations deserve special thanks: Richard Arnoff of Arnoff Moving & Storage; the DOT Internet discussion group; Stephanie Haimes of AAA; David Malsch of the Washington State DOT; Art Salazar of Caltrans; the New York State Thruway Authority, particularly David Ardman, Steve Fabbie, Roy Grisenthwait, and Tom Ferritto; Margaret Goldstein; and Mohamed Ben Jemaa

Library of Congress Cataloging-in-Publication Data

Whitman, Sylvia, 1961–
     Get up and go : the history of American road travel / Sylvia Whitman.
       p.   cm.
     Includes bibliographical references and index.
     Summary: Examines how people have traveled across the United States on roads from Indian trails to interstate highways and describes the development of different means of transportation and their impact on American society.
     ISBN 0-8225-1735-3 (alk. paper)
     1. Travel—United States—History—Juvenile literature. 2. Roads—United States—History—Juvenile literature. 3. Coaching—United States—History—Juvenile literature. 4. Railroads—United States—History—Juvenile literature. [1. Roads—History. 2. Travel—History. 3. Transportation—History.] I. Title.
HE325.W48   1996
388.1'0973—dc20   95-39694

Manufactured in the United States of America
1 2 3 4 5 6 - JR - 01 00 99 98 97 96

Contents

FOLLOWING IN INDIAN FOOTSTEPS

We wait in darkness!
Come, all ye who listen,
Help in our night journey:
Now no sun is shining;
Now no star is glowing;
Come show us the pathway.

—Iroquois Indians,
"The Darkness Song"

The New York State Thruway Authority, the agency that runs the longest toll superhighway in the United States, tries to stay on the cutting edge of road technology. In one experiment, workers have cut shallow grooves into the shoulders of the thruway: when sleepy drivers veer out of their lanes and over the grooves, noise and vibration wake them up. To keep roads from cracking and to keep down repair costs, crews are testing a fiber mesh placed between the layers of pavement. Since the thruway is a toll road, drivers must pay to use it. Commuters can now buy an E-ZPass, a credit-card-sized tag that lets them whiz through certain toll booths without stopping to pay. An antenna, hooked up to a computer, scans the tag on a car and deducts the toll from the driver's prepaid account. E-ZPass is part of a program to develop a "smart highway" that reduces traffic jams and pollution. Soon the thruway authority will embed sensors in the asphalt to track the flow of vehicles. Radio

Toll plaza at rush hour. Motorists must pay a user's fee on many American roadways. Opposite: eastern Carolina Indian, 18th-century lithograph

broadcasts and dashboard computers will alert drivers to tie-ups and suggest alternate routes. Under federal law, 10 percent of new cars must run on electricity by the year 2003, so the thruway authority plans to bury a power cable in the roadway. Electric cars will tap in and recharge their batteries as they zip along.

Do drivers notice such developments? Maybe at first. But people soon grow accustomed to the conveniences that roads offer. Roads crisscross our lives; they connect us. Roads enable grandparents to visit, birthday packages to arrive, and oranges from Florida to reach supermarkets in

Ohio in winter. Sometimes roads connect us to people we'd prefer not to meet. Without roads there would be no drive-by shootings, no hit-and-run accidents. Roads divide us too. They tempt us to leave behind friends and relatives in search of better jobs, sunnier weather, or simply adventure. Roads offer avenues of escape, as well as ways back home.

Still, Americans often take roads for granted. We travel them so much that we sometimes hardly see them. The next time you come to a road, look at it closely. What is it made of? Asphalt? Concrete? Brick? Dirt? Who is taking care of it—scattering salt on icy patches and scooping up dead squirrels? How is it marked? What sort of signs, buildings, and plants have grown up alongside the road? Can you guess how old it is? Who were the first people to use the road?

WALKING INDIAN FILE

The New York State Thruway officially opened on June 6, 1954, with about a fourth of its original 461 miles complete. Governor Thomas E. Dewey traveled in a motorcade to seven different highway interchanges, where local officials greeted him with much fanfare. The city of Syracuse, for instance, introduced "Little Miss Thruway," 12-year-old Sharon Hemings, who had won the title after 20,000 readers sent in ballots to the *Syracuse Post-Standard*. Also attending the ceremony were several chiefs representing the Iroquois League of Six Nations. They presented the governor with a beaded rug, illustrating the passage of the thruway through old tribal lands. For all of its state-of-the-art engineering, the most modern road in the United States at that time followed Native American footpaths thousands of years old.

Spread out across a continent, the Indian tribes of North America lived mostly independent of each other. Native Americans in the desert, plains, and forests had different lifestyles. Some farmed; some hunted. Some occupied one pueblo year-round, while others migrated seasonally.

Indians traveled by foot on land or by canoe on water, which was usually faster. Hunting, trade, and warfare made long overland journeys necessary at times. Herd animals such as deer and buffalo left a few trails that people could follow. But usually Indians scouted out the most efficient paths—dry, level, and straight.

When attacking or retreating, war parties sometimes took risky shortcuts on steep slopes. But hunters dragging home carcasses or families heading to winter camps usually followed easier routes. They avoided soggy valleys in spring, when melting snow pushed rivers over their banks, and treeless ridges in summer, when the sun scorched the earth.

Tribes on good terms with each other shared trails. Descended from Ice Age hunters who had tracked herds of caribou into present-day upstate New York, the Cayugas, Mohawks, Oneidas, Onondagas, and Senecas formed the Iroquois League of Five Nations (later, with the addition of the Tuscaroras, six nations). The path that linked the longhouses of this confederation became known as the Ambassadors Road. Iroquois diplomats used "the path" as a metaphor for the bond between the tribes.

This prehistoric rock staircase was part of a network of Indian roads in Chaco Canyon, New Mexico.

"To cause great boulders to fall into the path" implied a threat to break off relations. "To sweep the path clean" meant to eliminate problems in the way of friendship.

Since Native Americans passed down traditions orally, through spoken tales rather than through books, no written records exist of their early customs. But by the 1600s, Europeans had begun to settle in North America. Explorers and traders often enlisted Indian guides and hiked Indian paths. The Europeans' journals describe roads and travel in the New World.

Captured as a teenager during a raid on the Pennsylvania frontier in 1758, Mary Jemison grew up as an adopted daughter of the Seneca Indians. She discovered one reason that Native Americans kept a minimum of household goods—to travel light. "I learned to carry loads on my back, in a strap placed across my forehead," she told a writer years later.

According to botanist John Bartram, who collected plants up and down the East Coast in the 1700s, Native Americans traveled with a food called "parched meal." Before a trip, they browned corn in hot ashes; cleaned, pounded, and sifted it; then added sugar. On the trail, they mixed a quarter pint of parched meal with a pint of water to make a satisfying instant dinner.

Hungry hikers, whether European or Native American, rarely lost sight of wild game and fruit, from red plums to huckleberries. On the bank of Pennsylvania's Little Beaver Creek in 1772, explorer David McClure spotted geese, turkeys, and pigeons, "& all being within musket shot, we had our choice for a supper. My interpreter chose the Turkies, & killed three at one shot."

On busy routes, travelers often found rough shelters and cabins for spending the night or waiting out a rainstorm. Built by white and Indian hunters, these shelters sometimes contained a stock of bear meat. Strangers could usually expect hospitality in Indian settlements. European missionaries crossing Pennsylvania in the 1820s reported that Indians greeted travelers with an expression about pulling briars from their legs. Everyone understood the hardship of forest journeys.

Some tribes used a message system on the trail: they stripped a ring of bark from trees and painted pictures on the wood using red ochre and charcoal. Hunters recorded their kills; warriors left threats to intimidate their enemies. After Moravian missionaries began converting Delaware Indians to Christianity, Bible verses in the Delaware language sometimes appeared on trees near native villages. Traveling along the Mahoning Path toward Pittsburgh in 1789, Moravian Abraham Steiner described a tree painting in his diary:

> Here was a peeled tree on which some great warrior during the last war had inscribed his exploits with charcoal and red-stone. We got the Indians to interpret it for us. On one side 7 muskets had been painted, one on top of the other. This means that 7 warriors had gone to war from there. On the other side was a turkey to indicate that their leader was of the turkey tribe. Beside it were 8 thick diagonal lines one above another. This means that the chief had gone out on so many raids. In the lowest line were 4 arrows.... This means, each time the arrows were shown, that as many of them had been killed as there were arrows through the line.... Beside it lay 6 men one on top of another with their feet higher than their heads. This means that his party had killed so many white people.

Because it had so many of these early billboards, a section of the Towanda Path in central Pennsylvania was dubbed "the Painted Line."

NO PLACE FOR WANDERLUST

Colonists explored and settled along waterways. In the early 1700s, villages grew up near harbors, inlets, and rivers. Fast-growing cities—Boston, New York, Philadelphia, Charleston, Savannah—lined the East Coast. Settlers depended on the Atlantic Ocean for all trade, travel, and communication with Europe.

For protection, a settlement usually started out as a clearing within or near a fort. Colonists often duplicated city-planning patterns from their old countries. In the Southwest, Spaniards who moved north from Mexico followed the 1573 code of "Royal Ordinances for the Laying

Out of New Cities, Towns, or Villages." They arranged a grid of streets parallel to a central, rectangular plaza of shops, houses, and a church. New England towns centered around a "common" or a "green" with a religious meetinghouse. Paths radiated out to a ring of fields. In New Amsterdam (now New York City), a *breede weg,* or broad way, led out of the fort to a shared pasture for cows and sheep. But roads rarely extended beyond these self-sufficient farming communities. Many people were afraid of what lay outside: the dark, "howling wilderness" full of "savages."

As in European cities, local governments required men to spend a couple days a year laying out and maintaining roads within settlements—

Industrious settlers and Native Americans clear the wilderness in this imaginary scene of colonial Georgia.

chopping down trees, packing dirt and branches into holes. It was sweaty work. Yet the sometimes halfhearted labor of assorted citizens couldn't always keep up with the need for new routes, especially in cities. Six years after the founding of Boston, selectmen ordered two "street-ways" built, but the officials soon gave up trying to regulate road building and let individuals (often merchants) construct streets at their own expense.

Dirt paths slowly developed where people, animals, and carts passed regularly. These lanes wound and twisted, but they had charm. Sam Walter Foss described the evolution of Boston's Washington Street in "The Calf-Path" (1907):

One day, through the primeval wood,
A calf walked home, as good calves should;
But made a trail all bent askew,
A crooked trail, as all calves do . . . .
This forest trail became a lane
That bent and turned and turned again . . . .
And this, before men were aware,
A city's crowded thoroughfare . . . .
And men two centuries and a half
Trod in the footsteps of that calf.

As the population of the colonies grew, so too did the disorder. New York imposed a series of rules to improve routes within the settlement. A 1697 law directed every seventh household to put out a lantern on a pole "in the dark time of the moon, for the ease of the inhabitants." The seven neighbors in the vicinity split the cost—and anyone who refused to pay up faced a nine-pence penalty. Around that time, street cleaning

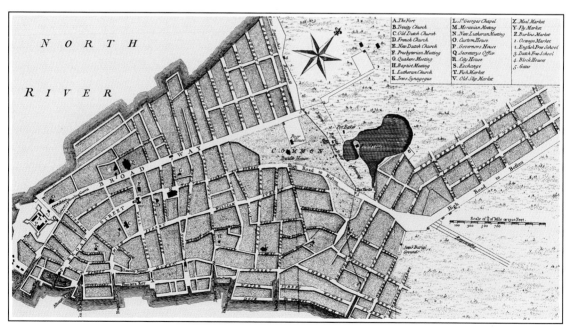

New York City, 1763. Broad Way led to a common where inhabitants grazed livestock.

began, and soon a cart came around on Fridays to collect the trash people swept out their front doors. Home owners paid six pence for the service, or half that if they shoveled the refuse into the cart themselves. City leaders also imposed a speed limit on horses within the city gates. No one was permitted to ride "faster than a foottap."

As communities sprawled over their original limits, roads eventually reached into the countryside. Colonists cut oaks and pines at a heedless clip. They used the lumber for house and ship construction, as well as for export. The woods were vast, though, and settlements remained islands in a sea of trees, boulders, and shrubs.

Settlers found boat travel much easier than land travel in the thickly wooded eastern part of North America. To cover long distances, they preferred to sail up and down the coast. But ships were often overbooked or delayed by storms and ice. So people braved other difficulties—traveling horseback on narrow Indian footpaths. Horses slogged through swamps and picked their way over fallen logs; riders didn't make much better time than hikers. After traveling from Boston to New York in 1704, a Madam Knight complained:

> The Rodes all along this way were very bad. Incumbered with Rocks and mountainos passages, which were very disagreeable to my tried carcass. In going over a Bridge, under which the River Run very swift, my hors stumbled and very narrowly 'scaped falling over into the water.

Both public and private post riders carried mail and newspapers between settlements. Traders guided trains of pack animals through the woods. As more immigrants arrived from Europe wanting farmland, families began migrating inland. Looking for fresh fields, they followed rough paths left by earlier travelers.

HITCHING A WAGON TO A STAR

Britain didn't consider road building a priority in its American colonies, nor did colonists want to pay more taxes. But two developments in the 1700s heightened interest in improved roads: commerce and the Conestoga wagon.

European colonists belonged to a capitalist society, which encouraged individuals to accumulate wealth—everything from pewter plates and linen tablecloths to mahogany cabinets and glass chandeliers. Buying and selling raw materials and finished products fueled the economy— and prompted freight service across New Jersey as early as 1707. Once every two weeks, a wagon carried goods between Philadelphia and New York.

But roads full of boulders and stumps ruined shipments. Boxes and barrels tumbled, wooden wheels cracked, and sometimes whole wagons rattled into pieces. In 1750, German farmers in the Conestoga Valley of Pennsylvania began making a sturdy vehicle to haul vegetables to Philadelphia and Baltimore. The covered Conestoga wagon gave a huge

Conestoga wagons hauled heavy loads.

boost to land travel. With its flared ends and its broad wheels four inches or more wide, it looked clumsy. But it held loads in place. Usually pulled by six horses, a Conestoga could transport at least three tons.

A Conestoga could lumber along at about two miles per hour—but only on the smoothest paths. Improving roads would speed up delivery. In the 1780s, Virginia, Connecticut, and Maryland began to charge tolls on some routes to pay for better surfacing.

Although Conestoga wagons dominated the road for only a century, they left a lasting imprint. The driver rode on the left side of the wagon, sometimes walking or standing on the "lazy-board," an oak plank between the two left wheels. From there, he could guide the horses and pull the long iron brake handle. To have a clear view ahead, the Conestoga teamster kept his wagon on the right side of the road. Other traffic took to following in the Conestoga's ruts—establishing the American custom of traveling on the right-hand side of the road.

In an age of growth and ambition, Conestogas gave wheels to American dreams. Benjamin Parker described himself as a child on the frontier of Indiana:

> With the tinkling of the [rig's] bells, the rumbling of the wheels, the noise of the animals, and the chatter of the people, as they went forever forward, the little boy who had gone down to the road from his lonesome home in the woods was naturally captivated and carried away into the great active world that he had not before dreamed of.

PROGRESS COMES DOWN THE PIKE

Coaches will be overloaded, it will rain, the dust will drive, baggage will be left to the storm, passengers will get sick, a gentleman of gallantry will hold the baby, children will cry, nature demands sleep, passengers will get angry, the drivers will swear, the sensitive will shrink, rations will give out, potatoes become worth a gold dollar each, and not be had at that.

—Demas Barnes,
From the Atlantic to the Pacific, overland, 1866

In the years leading up to the American Revolution, ideas as well as freight traveled rough East Coast roads. Pamphlets, newspapers, letters, preachers, merchants, drama troupes, and politicians circulated, spreading a conviction that the American colonies had more in common with each other than they did with Britain. During the Revolutionary War (1775–1783), soldiers marched, supply trains followed, and Paul Revere made his famous midnight ride on the roads that linked settlements. Yet the American army often waited hungrily for beef, rum, and supplies. Icy roads around Providence, Rhode Island, once delayed wagons full of flour for three weeks. Despite such obstacles, America eventually won independence from Britain.

Americans hit the road after the war. Sometimes they hit hard. According to the 1797 *American Annual Register,* stagecoaches struck potholes up to 10 feet deep on the route from Philadelphia to Baltimore and often overturned, killing passengers and disabling horses. Isaac Weld of Britain described a hair-raising ride in *Travels through the States of North America* (1799):

> The roads in this state [Maryland] are worse than in any one in Union; indeed so very bad are they, that on going from Elktown to the Susquehannah Ferry, the driver frequently had to call to the passengers in the stage, to lean out of the carriage first at one side, then at the other, to prevent it from oversetting in the deep ruts with which the road abounds: "Now, Gentlemen, to the right," upon which the passengers all stretched their bodies halfway out of the carriage to balance it on that side: "Now, Gentlemen, to the left," and so on.

The rough-and-tumble conditions in the United States often appalled foreign visitors. But where Europeans saw danger, squalor, and uncivilized wilderness, hopeful 19th-century Americans saw opportunities for progress.

STRAIGHT LINES FROM UNCLE SAM

Many American leaders recognized that reliable routes of communication, defense, and commerce would strengthen their newly formed nation. Unsure of its powers, however, Congress argued about whether it should build highways or simply designate the right-of-way—determine where roads would go. Since the United States had just fought to break free of a strong British government that imposed burdensome taxes, politicians hesitated to tax citizens for road construction. During Thomas Jefferson's presidency (1801–1809), he ordered improvements to the National Road, an established path from Cumberland, Maryland, to Zanesville, Ohio. Workers trimmed trees in the road to stumps—9 to 15 inches high—so wagons could pass over them. But the government shied away from bolder, more expensive road-building projects.

Congress did undertake one ambitious effort, however. In 1785, lawmakers authorized a survey of the American "backland"—the Midwest. Surveyors used a Gunter's chain, 66 feet long, to measure out square miles. Aligned north-south and east-west, each square mile, or section, contained 640 acres. A larger square, six miles long by six miles wide, formed a township. As the United States acquired vast new western territory through deals with other nations, wars, and squatting in the 19th century, surveyors continued to impose this grid. (In one swoop, the Louisiana Purchase of 1803 extended the country from the Mississippi River to the Rocky Mountains.) Today, seen from the air, two-thirds of the United States resembles a checkerboard.

The grid made it easier for lawmakers, census takers, mail carriers, tax collectors, and farmers to catalog the new territory and its people. Settlers built roads along section lines, with schools, churches, and stores located at the crossroads.

Although orderly, the grid did not work as perfectly on land as on paper. First of all, self-taught American surveyors sometimes made mistakes in their calculations. Secondly, traveling from place to place along

An 18th-century traffic accident. "Corduroy roads" and stagecoaches combined for a bruising trip.

the perimeter (outside edges) of a square took much more time than crossing on a diagonal. More miles of road meant more maintenance. And unlike a New England town, laid out like a wheel with hub and spokes, a community along the grid often had no obvious center. Finally, section lines ignored the natural contours of the land, climbing up mountains, cutting through swamps, and creating nightmarish routes for tired horses.

CONVENIENCE FOR SALE

Back east, private corporations stepped into the road-building business. To raise money for road construction, businesses sold stock. They charged tolls to users, paid back stockholders—and made a profit. In 1792 the Philadelphia and Lancaster Turnpike Company sold shares for $300 and spent two years building a crushed stone road at a cost of $7,500 for each of its 62 miles. Other companies soon followed. By 1838, almost 8,000 miles of turnpikes (toll roads) crisscrossed New York and New England. (The word *turnpike,* like *turnstile,* originally referred to a gate developed in England. A pole with four sticks radiating horizontally from its top allowed people, but not cattle, to pass through.)

States regulated turnpike companies since they performed a public service. Pedestrians paid almost nothing to use the roads, herders with their sheep and cows paid a little more, and vehicles—wagons and stagecoaches—paid the most. Frequent users, such as freight wagons, could arrange for discounts. In Massachusetts, a law exempted citizens from paying tolls on their way to church, family visits, military duty, or the gristmill.

States set construction standards, too. The English practice of topping gravel with broken stones worked the best but cost the most. So, many companies used just gravel or wooden planks to cover roads. Logs laid across the path created a "corduroy road," ridged like corduroy fabric. This surface made for bumpy rides but provided solid footing.

Stagecoaches, which carried passengers, and Conestogas, which carried freight, dominated turnpikes and highways. Entrepreneurs had launched stagecoach lines even before the Revolutionary War, but such businesses multiplied in the early 19th century. Drivers tried to keep to regular schedules along set routes and changed horses at intervals (stages). Gershom Johnson operated stagecoaches out of his Bunch of Grapes tavern in Philadelphia. He advertised a "convenient Flying Stage Waggon" with "four horses at the end of every twenty miles" on the twice-weekly run to Elizabeth, New Jersey. The fare started at four dollars, then rose to six dollars when the price of oats and hay went up.

Coach rides proved safer, faster, and more reliable than lone horseback rides through the woods. So, in 1785, Congress voted to use stagecoaches to carry mail. Stage owners offered special rates for newspaper delivery, and—until telegraphs came on line in the 1840s—news traveled mainly by road. Stagecoaches knit together the countryside. Rural folks often enlisted drivers to run errands in town. In the early days, stages delivered passengers to their doors.

Under the wear and tear of weather and traffic, road surfaces deteriorated quickly. Although profit-conscious companies didn't rush to invest in road repairs, Americans still noticed dramatic improvements. When blacksmith Levi Pease began building his stagecoach empire in 1783, his coaches traveled from Boston to New York in six days. By 1820, that trip took only 36 hours. Sleeker stagecoaches, which had evolved from flat wagons with benches, contributed to speed.

Since passengers often arrived bruised, carriage makers worked to make stagecoaches more comfortable. They added a roof, then leather curtains that rolled down to keep out dust and rain. To cushion the bumps, manufacturers tried slinging the coach on heavy leather straps attached to iron bars front and back. But that design created a sickening sideways sway and was eventually abandoned.

Most coaches carried 6 to 12 passengers, plus mail. Riders faced each other front and back, with a third row in the middle. Courteous gentlemen often invited ladies to the rear seat, the only one with back support. The driver rode outside, slightly lower than the roof, which held luggage and sometimes extra passengers.

New stagecoach models often took the name of the city in which they were manufactured. The most famous was the Concord coach, designed by Lewis Downing of Concord, Massachusetts. His coaches sold all over the country and as far away as Africa and Australia. When ordering a Concord coach, customers could specify color, a leather or plush interior, oil or candle lamps, even glass on doors.

Most proprietors wanted the name of their company painted on their coaches in ornamental letters—Pioneer, Good Intent, Oyster Line (which shipped shellfish from the Chesapeake Bay to Pittsburgh). Individual carriages had names too, such as Gentle Annie. Of course, passengers came up with their own nicknames: they referred to the Express Line, which averaged a whopping 11 miles per hour, as the Shake Gut.

DON'T LET THE BEDBUGS BITE

Travelers always needed food and shelter. In unsettled territory, pioneers stopped at traders' huts and army forts for refreshment and repairs. Welcoming news and diversion, many Americans on the frontier opened their homes to strangers passing through. "Farmers have generally a room appropriated to the reception of travelers, for whose food they charge moderately," wrote Englishman Elias Fordham as he crossed Indiana in 1817. Preachers and fellow homesteaders usually stayed for free.

As traffic increased, though, hospitality developed into a business. Tavern-inns opened along the road. Most inns started out as a cabin, with a blanket for a door and earthen floors where men and women slept side by side in their clothes. In 1789, a New Englander reported that guests at one western Pennsylvania lodge slept lined up like spoons; to turn on their sides, they had to roll all at once on cue. Slowly, inns added comforts like mattresses and private rooms. But even as late as the 1850s, only the best hotels provided individual washstands and chamber pots.

States often licensed tavern-inns. Sometimes owners needed to prove good moral character to get a license, and they always had to post their rates. Laws prohibited gambling and liquor sales to children, servants, and slaves. But hygiene didn't always concern the government or innkeepers. "Sir, two hundred men have wiped on that towel and you are the first to complain," a Missouri host told one guest.

In *Excursion through the Slave States,* Englishman George Featherston-haugh complained about dirty innkeepers and gritty meals. On that trip in the 1830s, Featherstonhaugh remembered "little pieces of pork swimming in hog's grease, some very badly made bread, and much worse coffee" in Arkansas. Breakfast could take hours to serve if the innkeep-er's wife had only a single skillet for frying—first bacon, then pancakes, then potatoes, then eggs.

Travelers needed tolerance, since they shared everything from lice to outhouses. All classes of people rubbed elbows at roadside inns—judges, actors, preachers, migrating families. Although wagon drivers often camped outside on a "Tucson bed" (a roll of straw covered with carpet), they too gathered at tavern-inns for hot meals, beer, and evenings of cards, checkers, and fiddle music. On her way from Connecticut to Ohio in 1810, Margaret Van Horn Dwight spent a night at an inn "fill'd with half-drunken noisy waggoners . . . I can neither think nor write," she con-fided in her journal. One of them "makes so much noise with his love songs; I am every moment expecting something dreadful & dare not lay down my pen lest they should think me listening to them." But other Americans enjoyed the home-cooked meals and mixed company.

Burly freight drivers, uniformly dressed in wool hats, leather boots, and red flannel shirts, smoked thin cigars that sold four for a penny. Soon the whole country was calling these cheap smokes "stogies"— from the word *Conestoga.* Henry Lee Fisher reminisced in his 1888 poem "Wagoning":

> There was never a rougher set,
> Or class of men upon the earth,
> Than wagoners of the Reg'lar line,
> Nor jollier when in their wine . . . .
> Around the blazing hearth at e'en,
> Or roaring ten-plate Pinegrove stove,
> Those heroes of the turnpike-roads—
> Those haulers of the heavy loads,
> Or weary drivers of a drove,
> Forgathered many a winter's night
> In freedom, fun, and fond delight.

To no one's surprise, many wagoners married daughters of innkeepers on their regular routes.

Although inns also served local communities—hosting dances, cornhuskings, and even treaty negotiations—owners understood that their livelihood depended on through traffic. When Lemuel Jackson was building an inn in Michigan in 1830, he took a break to lobby lawmakers in Detroit, pressing them to route the territorial road through his town. Inns put up gaudy signs. One on the National Road featured a barmaid holding a jug; liquor arced from it into a glass held by George Washington.

Both Levi Pease and Gershom Johnson started inns, then guaranteed extra business by adding stage service. Other proprietors cut deals to make sure coaches full of hungry, exhausted travelers arrived at their doors. One inn charged stage lines $500 a year to feed their horses and drivers—but only $350 if the line scheduled a meal stop for the passengers. Folks in the country grew used to the sound of horns tooting as stagecoaches approached a tavern. Drivers honked once for every traveler who planned to eat dinner.

The Phoenix Line advertised "Safety Coach" service between Washington, D.C., and Baltimore. The 37-mile trip took five hours.

Mud and washed-out bridges might strand guests for days. So some innkeepers didn't mind lousy roads. But most pushed for improvements. Better access meant more business.

"POOR PADDY WORKS ON THE RAILWAY"

Then the train whistle blew. By the mid-19th century, the "iron horse" had pulled traffic off roads like a magnet. The earliest trains looked like linked stagecoaches. Railroad cars soon became comfortable cabins, however, with dining and sleeping rooms. Steel tracks allowed for smooth, fast rides. While stagecoaches left before dawn to cover as much ground as possible in daylight, trains departed and arrived at more convenient hours—with fewer delays. Soon the federal government was granting land and rights-of-way to railroad companies. Highways fell into disrepair, taverns closed, and Conestogas gave way to short-haul wagons.

In the wide-open West, though, stagecoaches continued to operate through the end of the century. In 1865, New York businessman Demas Barnes rode stages from the Midwest to California to check out mining opportunities. "It is not a *pleasant,* but it is an *interesting* trip," he wrote to his associates in one of several letters published in the *Brooklyn Eagle.*

Barnes took the train as far as Atchison, Missouri, then boarded the overland stage. The 640-mile run from Atchison to Denver took six and a half days. Often the stage forded streams: "At the crossing of the big Blue creek, the driver put our feet bout one foot under water without notice, and thought it a good joke."

Near Denver, fearing Indian attack, the stage driver picked up an escort of soldiers. With white Americans pushing westward, breaking treaties, and in some cases slaughtering Indians, many tribes were hostile to travelers. But Barnes suspected "the soldiers plundered and stole more than the Indians." Between Denver and Salt Lake City, the threat of Indian attack delayed the stage several times. It no longer traveled at night. At one point, Indians killed a cavalry soldier, "leaving one bullet in his head and eight arrows through his body." The sight didn't disturb Barnes too much; he kept one of the arrows as a souvenir.

Continuing his journey through Nevada, he complained again about

After the "golden spike" ceremony at Promontory, Utah, railroads crossed the nation coast to coast.

his fellow passengers, this time a widow with four children who were "covered with molasses" and dropping crumbs on the seats. The leg over the snowcapped Rockies frightened him, since two men had died in an avalanche as they tried to open the road during the winter. But Barnes reached San Francisco without injury, pleased with his adventure and excited by the investment possibilities in the West. He knew that laborers (mostly Chinese and Irish immigrants) were laying ties for a transcontinental railroad that would open up new markets nationwide.

In 1869, at Promontory, Utah, the Union Pacific and the Central Pacific railroads hammered the final, golden spike of the coast-to-coast track. Whereas roads had merely extended commerce and communication, the railroad would revolutionize them. The Reverend John Pierpont Morgan, grandfather of railroad king J. P. Morgan, expressed an older generation's sense that this change also brought loss:

> We hear no more the clanking hoof,
> And stage-coach rattling by;
> For the steam-king rules the traveled world,
> And the pike is left to die.

TRAVELING UNDER THEIR OWN STEAM

*Afoot and light-hearted I take to
    the open road,
Healthy, free, the world before me,
The long brown path before me
    leading wherever I choose ....
You road I enter upon and
    look around,
I believe you are not all that
    is here,
I believe that much unseen is
    also here.*

    —Walt Whitman,
    "Song of the Open Road," 1856

Although Americans depended on public transportation for long-distance journeys through the 19th century, they also liked the freedom of coming and going at will. Near home, most folks rode horses or walked. Wealthier Americans indulged in all sorts of private carriages.

"Some talk about my buying a shay," the Reverend Joseph Emerson of Malden, Massachusetts, wrote in his diary in 1735. He was referring to the popular Yankee shay, a variation of the English chaise. This two-wheeled, horse-drawn chair sometimes sported a collapsible hood. "How

Kid-sized carriage, Santa Fe, New Mexico

much reason have I to watch and pray and strive against inordinate affection for the Things of the World," he wrote. It didn't take long, however, for temptation to overcome restraint. A week later, the minister bought his shay.

PRAIRIE SCHOONERS ON A SEA OF GRASS

Simple chairs and fancy coaches couldn't survive a long-distance road trip, and they remained a city luxury through the 1870s. Farmers relied on wagons. So did the hundreds of thousands of Americans who headed to the advancing frontier to claim a homestead or to pan for gold.

"Go West, young man," wrote Horace Greeley in a *New York Herald Tribune* editorial in the 1850s, "and grow up with the country." Politicians joined him in encouraging white settlers to populate North America from sea to sea. The United States had entered an economic depression in 1837. Wages fell and banks closed. Easterners and midwesterners who felt trapped in crowded cities or on worn-out farmland eagerly swapped trappers' reports and settlers' journals describing the rich soil of Oregon and California.

The opening of these new territories enticed more than 250,000 emigrants to brave a journey on the Overland Trail between 1840 and 1870. From the relative comfort and safety of his stagecoach, Demas Barnes admired the procession:

> The wagons have high boxes, covered with white canvas drawn over high wooden bows. As they wind their slow course over the serpentine roads and undulating surface in the distance . . . the effect is poetic, grand, beautiful.

The view from within the wagon trains was much less glamorous. Many folks kept a diary, either as a souvenir of the trip or as a travel aid for friends to follow. These writings document a trail of hardships, accidents, and disease.

In winter, emigrants gathered at "jumping-off places" along the Missouri River, such as Independence or St. Joseph. Using savings or proceeds from the sale of a farm, they outfitted their covered wagons. By the 1850s, Conestogas were disappearing. Emigrants preferred a plain flatbed wagon that cost about $400. It was a big expense, but cost less than stagecoach fare for a whole family (Demas Barnes paid $350 for his ticket from Missouri to Utah). Railroads didn't yet cover the territory.

To prepare for river crossings, families caulked the wagon with tar, carried in a bucket hung on the wagon's side. Following the suggestions of guidebooks and salesmen, they laid in supplies: heavy rope, water barrels, spare wheels, rifles. *The Emigrants Guide to Oregon and California* (1845) advised carrying 200 pounds of flour, 150 pounds of bacon, 10 pounds of coffee, 20 pounds of sugar, and 10 pounds of salt per person. Merchants often took advantage of demand and raised prices, especially as spring—departure season—neared.

Covered wagons on the Santa Fe Trail

Families who left in mid-April, after the snow melted, fared better on the 2,400-mile journey than latecomers. The early starters found un-muddied water holes and precious firewood. Their oxen grazed new grass. (Horses weren't hardy enough to pull wagons such a long distance.) To make the most of daylight, small groups of wagons set out early in the morning and camped by late afternoon, preferably near a stream. Everyone had jobs. Men swam the cattle and soaked the wooden wagon wheels; women gathered weeds and buffalo dung for cooking fires, then prepared dinner; children helped parents.

Although emigrants sometimes hired guides, usually they followed wheel ruts of earlier travelers, landmarks listed in guidebooks, and directions painted or carved on rocks. But people still got lost, especially when promises of a shortcut tempted them to peel off from the established trail. Lucy Hall Bennett, who crossed the continent at age 13, remembered that her wagon train split up, and half the group took a cutoff toward Oregon:

> The road we took had been traveled by the Hudson Bay Fur traders, and while it might have been alright for pack horses, it was certainly not adapted to immigrants traveling by ox train. The water was bad, so full of alkali you could hardly drink it. There was little grass and before long our cattle all had sore feet from traveling over the hard sharp rocks. After several of our party died, the men discovered that Meek [the man who had suggested the route] really knew nothing about the road.

A pioneer family stops to cook dinner in the Rockies.

Wagon trains sometimes stopped for provisions at army forts. As communities grew up along the route, emigrants found more services and supplies. By 1856, Salt Lake City boasted community bathhouses and barbershops. In the early years, Native Americans helped travelers, often making a little money by running ferries across rivers. Relations with Indians deteriorated, however, as settlers grabbed tribal lands. Emigrants feared Indian raids, one of many hazards along the road.

Travelers also suffered snakebites and broken legs, and earaches and fevers from sleeping under wagons in rainy weather. One diarist described pancake dough black with mosquitoes, which often spread malaria. Other deadly diseases included typhoid, smallpox, dysentery, and cholera. "The dead lay sometimes in rows of fifties or more," wrote Ezra Meeker, describing a scene along the Platte River in the 1850s. "Crowds of people were continually hurrying past us in their desperate haste to escape."

When men drowned or children were pitched out of the wagons and got run over, the family had to bury them and move on. "The heart has a thousand misgivings, and the mind is tortured with anxiety," wrote Lodisa Frizell, a mother of four, in 1852. "And often as I have passed the fresh made graves, I have glanced at the side boards of the wagons, not knowing how soon it would serve as a coffin for some one of us."

Mothers felt the losses and hardships of the journey keenly. They missed the comfort and the company of home, especially since one out of five women was traveling while pregnant. But some women shared in the excitement of fresh starts and adventures on the road. Driving the oxen gave teenager Mary Ellen Todd "a secret joy in being able to have a power that set things going."

The final leg of the journey always tested the mettle of travelers. Exhausted and low on supplies after at least six months on the trail, they raced to get over the Rockies and the Sierras before snow blocked mountain passes. Sometimes the path was so narrow and steep that travelers disassembled wagons and pulled the pieces over the peaks with ropes. To lighten the load for animals, people walked. After carrying two of her seven children through snow, mud, and water up to her knees in 1847,

Eliza Smith Geer wrote in her journal, "I was so cold and numb I could not tell by feeling that I had any feet at all . . . . I have not told you half we suffered."

MAIN STREETS

Once people settled, they unhitched oxen and harnessed horses. All across the United States, horse traffic shaped the sights, sounds, and smells of small towns. Hitching posts marked parking spots. Thirsty animals—including pigs and sheep herded through town—drank at watering troughs. Main street had to be wide enough for a farmer to turn around his team and wagon. On side lanes, livery stables provided hay and shelter for horses. Doctors often kept rigs there so they could head out on house calls. Funeral homes stabled their hearses. Nearby, blacksmiths pounded out horseshoes. The clanging of iron on anvil blended into the clopping of hooves, the cracking of whips, the buzzing of flies over steaming horse dung.

In crowded cities, residents complained about the din of traffic. Worse yet was the stink of dung and dead horses whose owners couldn't, or wouldn't, pay to have them hauled away when they collapsed on the job.

Pigs and other animals—here en route to the butcher shop—were a common sight on 19th-century streets.

Wagon traffic, pedestrians, fruit vendors, and other peddlers crowd into New York's Mulberry Street in the early 1900s.

Hooves kicked up so much dust that towns sent out horse-drawn sprinkler wagons to dampen dirt streets in summer. In winter, horses pulled wooden rollers, flattening the snow for sleighs. In spring, after mud reached the right consistency, horses dragged graders, smoothing and packing the roadway.

Over time, townspeople planted trees along residential streets. They paved sidewalks with concrete and streets with brick. Wealthy urban areas experimented with the latest paving technology. Passing through Chicago in 1865, a traveler noted the fine pavement—"smooth, ornamental, clean, and, what [roads] are intended for, noiseless and easy for horses." Professional road builders saturated foot-long wooden planks with hardener, placed them on a concrete foundation, then filled in the seams with a cement called macadam. (Macadam took its name from Scottish engineer John McAdam, who broke with tradition to pave with small instead of large limestone rocks. The limestone dust mixed with

Instead of paying a tax, this farmer contributes his team and his time to a spring road-grading effort.

water to create cement. American engineers made waterproof macadam out of stones bound with tar or asphalt.)

In much of the country, instead of paying a road tax, residents did most construction work themselves. Although towns were supposed to hire a professional road master, usually the most senior citizen supervised. Writing for *Scribner's Magazine* in 1889, geologist N. S. Shaler called this amateur effort a "picnic":

> Arriving on the ground long after the usual time of beginning work, the road-makers proceed to discuss the general question of road-making and other matters of public concern, until slow-acting conscience convinces them that they should be about their task. The volunteers plastered the road with mud, cleaned out a few drainage ditches, and, after a long lunch, knocked off early in the afternoon.

Yet small-town residents appreciated road improvements. When the post office began sending letter carriers door-to-door, cities erected street signs. Other businesses made home deliveries too. Dairy farmers dropped off milk. Coal companies brought fuel. In 1905 the public library in Washington County, Maryland, dispatched a horse-drawn bookmobile.

PEDAL PUSHERS

Thanks to the efficiency of railroad service over long distances, few Americans cared if highways deteriorated. But a new hobby changed attitudes. In the 1870s, Colonel Albert A. Pope, a Civil War veteran, began importing self-propelled transportation machines from England— bicycles. Soon he was manufacturing an American version, and, in 1887, he opened a bike shop in Boston. As the fad swept cities in the Northeast, cyclists lobbied for smoother roads.

Biking appealed to a generation that was discovering the joys and benefits of exercise. Unlike horses, bicycles needed no feeding or grooming. Women could ride them in long skirts, although some women challenged tradition by wearing calf-length pants called pedal pushers. Because the first American bikes cost $150 to $200, usually only the rich bought them. However, mass manufacturing soon lowered the price to about $30. One popular song from the 1890s captured the bicycle's promise of fun and freedom, even for a young couple without much money:

> Daisy, Daisy, tell me your answer do!
> I'm half crazy, all for the love of you!
> It won't be a stylish marriage;
> I can't afford a carriage.
> But you'll look sweet
> Upon the seat
> Of a bicycle built for two.

Not everyone appreciated the romance of this newfangled vehicle. Walkers and horseback riders accused cyclists of scorching (speeding) and scaring animals. As city dwellers pedaled into the countryside on weekends, they met hostility, suspicion, and harassment. At least one

American cyclists joined together and pushed for smoother roads.

rural county passed a law requiring cyclists to dismount when approaching a horse.

Bike lovers banded together. They sponsored races and read magazines such as *Wheel* and *Good Roads,* financed in part by Colonel Pope. The most prominent cycling club, the League of American Wheelmen, vowed "to ascertain, defend, and protect the rights of wheelmen [and] to encourage and facilitate touring." Founded in stylish Newport, Rhode Island, in 1880, the league contributed to the image of biking as a sport for the idle rich. Its suggestion that government spend tax dollars to improve roads faced stiff resistance at first.

However, cyclists enlisted allies across the nation. Railroads, wanting access to small towns, knew that blacktopping roads often cost less than building branch railroad lines. Paved roads encouraged people to ship freight all year long, not just in warm, dry months when muddy paths hardened. A powerful voting bloc, farmers disliked taxes. Yet they too realized that better feeder roads to railways would help them take crops to market. All these forces joined to found the National League for Good Roads, which spurred the creation of the federal Office of Road Inquiry in 1893. As the post office phased in Rural Free Delivery (mail service to scattered farmhouses), the Good Roads movement got another boost. All-weather routes meant prompt mail.

Limited by a modest $10,000 budget, the Office of Road Inquiry gathered information and educated the public. According to its 1904 census, the United States had more than two million miles of highway. But 93 percent of that length was dirt road. State-of-the-art asphalt covered only 18 miles; brick, 123 miles. Paving for the rest consisted of planks, shells, sand, and gravel.

Bicyclists continued to lead the way for better transportation. Developed for bikes, pneumatic rubber tires slowly replaced wooden wheels on most vehicles. Filled with compressed air, pneumatic tires provided a softer ride and did less damage to road surfaces. Meanwhile, inventors in Europe and the United States experimented with gears and engines. They created steam- and gas-powered tricycles, quadricycles, and "horseless carriages"—automobiles.

Lucius D. Copeland and his steam-powered tricycle, 1855

After reading about German Karl Benz's breakthroughs with gasoline engines in *Scientific American,* bicycle mechanics Charles and Frank Duryea of Massachusetts rigged a motor inside a buggy. The vehicle crashed into a wall. But the brothers kept tinkering, even though they ran out of money, and starvation sent Frank into the hospital for a time. In 1895, they entered another gasoline-powered buggy in a much publicized 55-mile race organized by the *Chicago Herald-Tribune.* The car won—one of only two finishers.

Although "the Duryea" had averaged a mere five miles per hour over icy Illinois roads, the car inspired automobile fans. Other Americans simply shrugged. They saw automobiles as expensive windup toys for the rich—sometimes funny, sometimes sinister, nearly always annoying. Sputtering and honking, cars spewed foul fumes, stalled at intersections, disturbed the peace, and ran over dogs and into fences. "Get a horse!" hecklers yelled.

This scorn didn't last long, though. Professor George Stewart remembered that the first car to enter his small Pennsylvania town around 1903 excited all the boys in the neighborhood. "My father and I happened to drive a little way out of town in a buggy," Stewart recalled in *U.S. 40,* "and he pointed out to me in the dust of the road a broad mark, broader than would be made by the ordinary wagon-wheel. That, he said, was the mark of the new automobile." Within two decades, even the hecklers would be driving one.

The victorious Duryea brothers after the Chicago race, 1895

ENGINE OF CHANGE

Come away with me, Lucile—
In my merry Oldsmobile,
Down the road of life we'll fly
Automobubbling, you and I.

              —Vincent Bryan,
   "In My Merry Oldsmobile," 1905

Like bicyclists, motorists united in the face of opposition. In 1902, there were 17 million horses on the road and only 23,000 cars. But drivers had already formed 50 auto clubs. What they lacked in numbers, they made up for in enthusiasm.

Early auto clubs drew members from the urban elite. When William Metzger opened a car dealership in Detroit in 1898, he sold his first 20 "mobile steamers" to four "capitalists," four doctors, four merchants, three "general businessmen," two manufacturers, one broker, one printer, and one plumber. Like golf and tennis, the "sport" of automobiling served a social function. On weekends, auto clubs held races and "reliability runs," in which drivers traveled leisurely over set routes to prove that cars provided dependable transportation.

They didn't. But at least drivers in a group could count on help and spare parts when spark plugs fizzled, radiators leaked, transmissions jammed, and tires blew out. Even wealthy motorists had to crank the starter and get their hands dirty under the hood.

To discourage traffic, some country towns let signposts fade and pot-holes deepen. Local sheriffs fined drivers for exceeding speed limits—eight miles per hour in some places. In other towns, a driver who didn't alert residents to an approaching car—by having someone walk in front waving a red flag—might be ticketed for negligence. So great was the fear of "explosive" combustion engines that motorists had to drain their gas tanks to cross a river by ferry. To pass from one state into another, drivers needed new licenses—and often new license plates. Auto clubs evolved into service organizations; club members warned each other about ridiculous regulations, speed traps, and innkeepers who charged outrageous prices for gas.

A MUDDY RIDE TO THE GOLDEN GATE

The Maxwell-Briscoe Company was looking for a way to publicize the safety and practicality of its automobiles when a sales manager spotted 20-year-old Alice Huyler Ramsey at an endurance run. President of the Women's Motoring Club of New Jersey, Ramsey handled her sporty, red, Maxwell roadster with confidence. (It was a gift from her lawyer husband, Bone, who never in his life got behind the wheel of a

Carriages and autos drove side by side at the turn of the century.

car.) The company proposed a deal: if it provided a car and paid her expenses, how would Ramsey like to become the first woman to drive cross-country?

With Bone's blessing, Ramsey agreed. She left their baby with a nurse-maid and set out on June 9, 1909, from the Maxwell-Briscoe showroom in Manhattan. Traveling with her were two older sisters-in-law and a friend, none of whom could drive.

The car, a Maxwell 30, was built for touring. The body rode high off the ground on big tires, and a metal pan underneath protected the engine from road damage. At night, Ramsey lit brass oil lamps on the hood. To turn on the headlights, she dropped carbide pellets into a generator, added drops of water, then struck a match. Although mechanics had installed a fuel tank that held 20 gallons instead of the usual 14 for this extraordinary trip, the car had no gas gauge. No windshield either. To protect their eyes from flying grit, Ramsey and her passengers wore goggles. And like most female motorists, Ramsey's crew traveled in long skirts, dusters (light overcoats), and hats with stiff visors—tied with crepe de chine veils knotted under their chins. Although the Maxwell had a convertible roof, it didn't ward off sun or rain very effectively. Leaving New York in the rain, the four women wore full body ponchos.

They motored north to Poughkeepsie, then west across the country. Maxwell-Briscoe hired the auto editor of the *Boston Herald* as a public relations advance man. He traveled mostly by train, booking hotel rooms and making sure crowds greeted the dirt-caked automobile at almost every stop. As Ramsey recalled in her memoir, *Veil, Duster, and Tire Iron,* one farm woman in a sunbonnet parked her wagon and team of horses along a section line, waiting for the foursome to arrive. "I read about you in the paper," she said, "and I've come six miles to see you."

Heavy rains in Iowa washed out bridges and turned highways into muddy lanes. The foursome spent a night in the car, waiting for swollen Weasel Creek to subside. Yet Ramsey resisted suggestions to ship her vehicle part of the way by railroad. She put her passengers on a train instead, lightening her load, and on her own took a longer, drier route through Iowa.

Reunited, the women crossed Nebraska, Wyoming, Utah, and Nevada. Roads and services petered out in the West. Their *Blue Book* road guide offered sketchy directions only from the East Coast to Missouri, so they had to follow wagon tracks. When the Maxwell hit a prairie dog hole in Utah, it lost a critical bolt in the tie-rod connecting the wheels. Luckily, Ramsey was able to wire the tie-rod together and creep to a nearby ranch for further repairs. Calling upon her skills as a mechanic as well as a driver, she coaxed her battered vehicle across desert and over mountains.

Weary but triumphant, the four women motored into San Francisco on August 10. They had crossed 3,800 miles in 41 days, using 11 spare

Alice Ramsey at the wheel

tires. Along with many other endurance runs, hill climbs, and reliability tests, Ramsey's journey helped convince Americans that they could depend on automobiles to take them wherever they wanted whenever they wanted.

"FIFTEEN KISSES ON A GALLON OF GAS"

Sniffing profits, many entrepreneurs leaped into the auto business. Henry Ford led the pack. Born on a Michigan farm, Ford repaired and installed steam engines in farm machinery as a young man, then worked as chief engineer for the Detroit Automobile Company. He struck out on his own with a vision of making cars for ordinary folks:

> I will build a motorcar for the great multitude. It will be large enough for the family but small enough for the individual to run and care for. It will be constructed of the best materials . . . but it will be so low in price that no man making a good salary will be unable to own one—and enjoy with his family the blessing of hours of pleasure in God's great open spaces.

Sequoia National Park "tree tunnel," 1907

In 1908 Ford produced a basic Model T—still pricey at $850. It came in one color: black. He shaped the body out of a steel alloy popular in Europe; it was tough enough to withstand thumps on American roads but light enough not to overtax the engine. Since rattling over ruts usually shattered glass windows, Ford hung curtains of transparent gelatin from the roof. These could be rolled up in nice weather. Hand-built European luxury cars usually had custom-made parts. But Ford and other American manufacturers standardized bulbs, belts, and spark plugs, so motorists could buy them anywhere and repair their own cars.

Ford also pioneered the assembly line. Instead of building an entire car from start to finish, workers specialized, assembling one section of the car as it traveled past them on a conveyor belt. This system sped up production and saved money. The price of a Model T, nicknamed the Tin Lizzie, dropped to $490 in 1914 and eventually below $300. Easy payment terms encouraged buyers. They made a 20 percent deposit, then paid the balance over a year.

Henry Ford's assembly line system meant more cars and cheaper cars for American consumers.

Horses were far from obsolete during the early automobile years. For more than one motorist, horses provided emergency towing service.

Songwriters sensed romance in the invention. Inspired by the trip of two Oldsmobiles from Detroit to Portland, Oregon, in 1905, Vincent Bryan and Gus Edwards composed a catchy tune about Johnnie Steele winning his girl Lucile in his Oldsmobile: "He lets her steer while he gets her ear." The waltz was such a hit that manufacturer Ransom Olds presented the two songwriters with a free car.

Children's books also capitalized on the public fascination with automobiles. In 1906, Stratemeyer Syndicate published *The Motor Boys Overland.* In a series of 22 books, the Motor Boys—Ned, Bob, and Jerry—traveled the world by motorcycle, car, powerboat, and flying machine, squaring off against their rival Noddy Noxious. Women were driving too. The Motor Boys were soon competing for readers against the Motor Girls, the Auto Boys, the Motor Maids, and the Automobile Girls. At first, writers cast these characters from upper-class families. But as car ownership spread, kids from all backgrounds were soon driving through the pages.

*Children's books offered
on-the-road adventures.*

Silent movies of the era, full of quick and silly car chases, made driving look even more fun and easy. In real life, however, even competent motorists spent a lot of time in ditches, bushes, and traffic. One postcard summed up a driver's "Motor Car Meditations":

> Hotly burns my rising ire,
> I am thoroughly disgusted;
> For I've lost a brand-new tire,
> And my steering gear has busted . . .
>
> Though upon the dusty road
> I kill no son or daughter,
> I flatten out full many a toad
> And hens I often slaughter.

City drivers faced other problems: no place to park and confrontations with horses, trolleys, electric "interurban" trains, and other motorists. Between 1900 and 1910, the number of cars in the United States leaped 1,600 percent. The distance of paved roads increased only 200 percent.

A DRIVE FOR FEDERAL FUNDING

In 1901, the National Good Roads Association loaded a train with reporters and road experts for a publicity tour to 16 cities. At each stop, construction crews built a sample mile or so of road—made of earth, stone, and gravel. Momentum was building—slowly—for large-scale improvements.

As the price of cars began dropping, auto club membership broadened. In 1902 nine local clubs formed the American Automobile Association (AAA), which signed up 10,000 members in less than a decade. The AAA printed maps, campaigned for uniform motor vehicle laws, and distributed information about garages, hotels, and highway conditions. It also joined the Good Roads movement.

Laying macadam pavement in Tennessee

Auto businesses—from tire manufacturers to oil companies—supported paving and extending routes, of course. Carl Fisher, the dashing founder of the Prest-O-Lite headlight company, complained, "The highways of America are built chiefly of politics, whereas the proper material is crushed rock, or concrete." In 1911, he bricked a local racetrack, creating the Indianapolis Speedway. A year later, he hosted a dinner for auto bigwigs and proposed private construction of a 3,150-mile road from New York to San Francisco: the Lincoln Highway. He appealed to businesses in cities along the route to help shoulder the expense of local sections. Over more than a decade, the Lincoln Highway emerged piece by piece.

Most roadway designers were engineers—often trained in the military, which always needed forts, bridges, and supply routes. After the Civil War, many army engineers ended up in state highway departments. They made do with tiny budgets funded by taxes, driver's license fees, and car registration fees. Over time, though, these engineers exerted a powerful influence. They formed the American Association of State Highway Officials, lobbying for road improvements and setting professional standards for construction.

Civil War veteran and engineer Roy Stone headed the federal Office of Road Inquiry. He envisioned steel roads—durable but much too expensive. Another engineer, geologist Logan Page, set up the first national roads material lab. He experimented with mixtures of oil, cement, concrete, brick, and slag, looking for the cheapest pavement that could withstand water, cold, and repeated poundings by vehicles that weighed several tons. As head of the Office (later Bureau) of Public Roads, Page trained a whole generation of highway engineers.

The federal government was inching toward leadership in building roads. Farmers opposed "peacock alleys," long-distance highways for city people showing off in their pleasure vehicles. But Roy Stone pushed for improved highways, arguing that rural Americans were already paying a "mud tax" of wasted time and money when their wagons bogged down on the way to market.

Automobiles proved their worth after the massive San Francisco earthquake of 1906. As fires raged, officials pressed private cars into service to evacuate the wounded. Shock waves had uprooted railroad tracks. So Walter White, head of the White Motor Company, organized a truck convoy to bring supplies to the devastated city. That year Henry Ford declared, "The automobile, while it may have been a luxury when first put out, is now one of the absolute necessities of our later day civilization."

A decade later, with more than two million motor vehicles on the loose, Congress finally passed the Federal Road Aid Act. The act allocated $75 million—which states had to match—to set up state highway departments and improve rural post roads.

World War I delayed these projects, but it emphasized the need for highways and local roads. Americans read in newspapers about taxis and cars racing troops and nurses from Paris to the front lines in 1914. As the fighting in France continued, ambulances (many driven by Americans) hurried maimed soldiers to hospitals, and trucks supplied battalions dug into their trenches.

World War I ambulance corps. In wartime, cars and trucks became a necessity.

By the time President Woodrow Wilson committed the United States wholeheartedly to the war in 1917, railroads couldn't meet the demand for transportation. Weapons plants needed shipments of steel. Arms, food, men, and army vehicles needed to reach the East Coast on the way to Europe. The auto industry, based mainly in Detroit, organized truck convoys to help out. But ruts, snow, and mud delayed these motorized wagon trains during a severe winter. Fifty thousand new trucks, destined for the battlefield in France, arrived too late to be of much use. Traffic jammed on inadequate roads around factories and seaports.

In 1921, Wilson signed into law the Federal Highway Act, which increased federal funds for state highway projects. Engineer Thomas MacDonald, appointed to lead the Bureau of Public Roads after Logan Page died of a heart attack, soon earned the nickname "Mr. Highways." He devised a uniform road numbering system: odd-numbered roads running north-south; even numbers running east-west. MacDonald also created the Highway Education Board, which sent speakers into schools, sponsored essay contests on the value of good roads, and awarded full college scholarships. When the students grew up, MacDonald figured, they would vote for highway projects.

Although wagons still trundled past MacDonald's office on Pennsylvania Avenue, the automobile had already won over the public. Woodrow Wilson was the last U.S. president to ride to his inauguration in a horse-drawn carriage. As he noted on the campaign trail in 1917, motorists were using up roads "almost as fast as we can make them."

ACCELERATING INTO THE FUTURE

I think that I shall never see
A billboard lovely as a tree.
Indeed unless the billboards fall
I'll never see a tree at all.

—Ogden Nash,
"Song of the Open Road,"
1933

In the early 1920s, the husband and wife team of Helen and Robert Lynd tried a new approach to anthropology. Instead of studying an unfamiliar foreign culture, they researched everyday life in Muncie, Indiana. One local citizen thought they were wasting their time. "Why on earth do you need to study what's changing this country?" he asked. "I can tell you what's happening in just four letters: A-U-T-O!"

By the end of 1923, even in the small town of Muncie, there were two cars for every three families. In their book *Middletown* (1929), the Lynds reported that working-class as well as wealthy citizens considered cars essential. A mother of nine said she'd rather live without clothes than give up the family car. Another woman ranked it above food.

Motor vehicles reduced the isolation of rural Americans. Rural Free Delivery improved; farmers received newspapers and popular magazines like *Ladies Home Journal* and *Collier's* within days of city folks. State agricultural agents traveled from town to town offering advice about farming. Salesmen knocked on doors to demonstrate new products. Buses transported children to large district schools. Bookmobiles encouraged reading, although people sometimes mistook them for hearses. "The first books cars were painted darker colors and did not have glass doors," recalled one woman, "so they were usually taken for the 'dead wagon' and urged to pass on from the door where they had stopped."

But automobile owners didn't have to wait around for house calls. They could go to the library themselves. Patients could drive to the doctor's office and later to medical centers, where doctors, freed from travel, could spend more time treating the sick.

TIN CAN TOURISTS

The appeal of automobiles extended beyond their practical value in running errands. They gave Americans new choices. In 1923, Bureau of Public Roads chief Thomas MacDonald took his publicity campaign to

Rural Free Delivery: a letter carrier makes his rounds in York County, Maine.

the radio, another popular new machine. "Radio is free as air," he said, "and the open road is symbolic of freedom."

City residents could escape by car from stress, crowds, and pollution. On parkways artfully planted with trees and shrubs—such as the Bronx River Parkway near New York City—motorists enjoyed scenic vistas. In Muncie, the Lynds found that on sunny Sundays families often skipped church services and motored to a nearby lake.

Soon families were enjoying not just Sunday drives but weekends at the beach and vacations on the road—leisure activities once reserved for the upper class. Auto safety and comfort were steadily improving. Developments included hydraulic brakes (1920), auto insurance (1922), the Rand McNally national road atlas (1924), safety glass and windshields (1926), antifreeze that permitted year-round travel (1926), sunroofs and front wheel drive (1929), windshield wipers and house trailers (1930).

Mobility gave Americans a new appreciation of their own country, helping erase a national inferiority complex. The United States had long bowed to Europe. But during World War I, the wealthy had to cancel their usual European tours, and they began to discover the grandeur of the West and the warmth of the South. Motorists in Model Ts followed.

Writing for *The Outlook* in 1925, C. P. Russell described the parade of northeasterners heading to Florida in cars and trailers as a second gold rush. Some motorists wanted sun; others were investing in property, hoping that prices would skyrocket. Although a devastating hurricane ended the Miami land boom, the winter migration of "snowbirds" continued.

National parks also drew motorists. Through 1917, no more than 52,000 people a year visited Yellowstone. But by 1929, the annual count was up to 228,000. Americans visited the West with a sense of nostalgia for the frontier and for the Indian culture by then largely destroyed. Teaming up with hotel and restaurant king Fred Harvey, the Santa Fe Railway sold ride-drive vacation packages called "Indian Detours." A passenger with a transcontinental train ticket could add a three-day motor trip to the Taos Pueblo of New Mexico for $65. Individuals could hire a car with a chauffeur and guide for $100 a day. Among hundreds of thousands of "detourists" were Eleanor Roosevelt (soon to be first lady) and physicist Albert Einstein and his wife.

Advertisements for Indian Detours promised romantic adventure "off the beaten path." Yet Harvey made sure that guests didn't suffer. Buses with revolving, cushioned seats met passengers at the station. In the evening, an attentive staff set up tents with cots and dining halls with full table linen. Native Americans had mixed feelings about the detours. On one hand, visitors spent money on native crafts. On the other, tourists showed little respect for Indian traditions, frequently disregarding requests not to photograph sacred ceremonies, for example.

In other parts of the country, where cultures weren't clashing, locals appreciated auto tourists more. At first, gas station and grocery store owners opened free "camping grounds" to lure customers. Farmers rented space in fields. Private homes also posted signs offering rooms to tourists.

Harvey "detourists" visit the Santa Clara Pueblo, 1930.

Soon, enterprising locals were building cabins that resembled dog-houses—wooden shells over dirt floors. These "auto courts" raised rates as they added beds, tables, plumbing, and other comforts.

Motels (motor hotels) appeared in the early 1920s. Like auto courts, motels began as groups of freestanding cabins. But side-by-side rooms, strung together in one long building, proved easier to construct and clean. Before the boom in roadside restaurants, many motel rooms contained kitchenettes. Motel owners, usually families, took pains to create a homey exterior to attract passing motorists. In 1920, AAA published its first campground directory, followed by guides to garages, hotels, and motels.

Thomas MacDonald claimed that national highways fostered a "broad Americanism" that would have prevented the Civil War. He exaggerated—but auto courts and campgrounds did encourage motorists to mingle. On his jaunt to Florida, C. P. Russell visited a camp on the edge of a North Carolina cotton farm. He counted about 60 travelers, "including dogs, cats, and ukuleles," from nine different states. After pitching tents and cooking dinner, travelers shared stories "of inhuman hills, of unsuspected holes, of terrifying detours, of blow-outs and broken parts." Rumors circulated that some Georgians created mud holes in order to charge stuck motorists $10 for a mule rescue. On the whole, though, Russell believed that competition for tourist dollars inspired road improvements rather than booby traps.

GYPSY TRUCKERS

Truckers also patronized roadside businesses. In the 1920s, thanks to smoother roads and pneumatic tires, trucks began competing seriously with railroads. As cities grew, new businesses located farther from train depots. Trucks offered door-to-door delivery at cut rates.

Full of risks, trucking nonetheless offered tough, determined workers a shot at owning their own businesses. In Chicago, Jack Keeshin traded four wagon teams for a Grabowski truck and founded Keeshin Southwest Motor Company in 1918. Truckers learned by doing. Because of the distance between service stations, Keeshin had to carry extra chains,

Fred Harvey provided Cadillacs and other reliable cars for detourists, but reliable roads were another story.

jack shafts, wire, and a can of highly flammable ether to loosen the oil that congealed on his truck's crankcase. He tried to build a reputation for efficiency and reliability—no cinch on roads without asphalt. As Keeshin wrote in *No Fears, Hidden Tears: A Memoir of Fourscore Years:*

> When I would drive those trucks over cobbled streets, and over mud roads as well, I'd have to get off the seat and rub my back for fear my kidneys would fall out.

Mack truck, 1913

Once, carrying 18,000 pounds of Fig Newtons from Chicago, Illinois, to South Bend, Indiana, Keeshin's truck ground to a halt in a sand patch near a cemetery. He needed to keep going: the 90-mile trip was supposed to take six days. So Keeshin pulled up 25 gravestones and laid them under his wheels. Although the police caught him, he managed to deliver his cookies. By 1930, Keeshin owned 100 trucks and grossed $500,000 a year.

Independent drivers who owned their own trucks were called "gypsies." "Wildcats," truckers who drove dangerously or handled freight carelessly, gave the profession a somewhat shady reputation. But most gypsies obeyed the law. Lillie and Willard Drennan hauled for the Texas oil fields. When Willard died in 1929, Lillie supported the family as the first licensed female truck driver in the United States. To guarantee steady work, some gypsies affiliated with larger companies that arranged back hauls (return loads) and insured shipments.

SYMBOL OF THE MODERN AGE

By 1929, Americans were driving 26.5 million cars, trucks, and buses. The American auto industry had pulled way ahead of its European counterparts, manufacturing 85 percent of motor vehicles worldwide. Engineering marvels included the Holland Tunnel, which allowed people to drive *under* the Hudson River between Manhattan and New Jersey. On opening day in 1927, the nation's first "mechanically ventilated underwater vehicular tunnel" attracted 51,694 vehicles. Some motorists drove back and forth several times out of sheer wonder.

During the 1920s, the distance of paved roads in the United States doubled. Yet there were 38 motor vehicles for every mile of blacktop. To control the flow, cities hired traffic cops and set up traffic lights, stop signs, one-way streets, and parking lots. These innovations transformed cityscapes but didn't eliminate chaos and congestion.

A commission on social trends appointed by President Herbert Hoover reported the obvious: the car had swept the nation, influencing even thought and language. Cars showed up on the cover of *The Saturday Evening Post* and in the comic strip *Gasoline Alley*. According to an Ohio University study, students referred to unpopular girls as "oil cans" and "flat tires." To express admiration, people exclaimed, "It's a doozy!"—a reference to the Duesenberg brothers' sleek roadsters favored by movie stars.

Consumers continued to buy cars (as well as other appliances) on credit. The cost of a new car—about $600—represented an average annual salary. Someone who earned five to ten dollars a week, such as a department store clerk, needed a loan to buy one. Banks happily stretched out payment terms to collect more interest. A bit of a sourpuss, small-town banker William Ashdown confessed in a 1925 article in *Atlantic Monthly* that he disapproved of easy terms. Even more than the financial drain of car ownership, Ashdown objected to the airs cars gave working people. He complained that carpenters were living in suburbs and even

Detroit's first stoplight, 1914

his laundress came to work in a taxi. "The ease with which a car can be purchased on the time payment plan is all too easy a road to ruin," he wrote.

In the 1920s, carmakers and other business executives discovered the power of advertising: it increased sales. Ads made much of the car's color. "The deep green of the forest is peaceful, cheerful, refreshing," proclaimed Cadillac in its advertisements. Even stubborn Henry Ford forsook basic black for "Arabian sand" and the like on his Model A's.

Ads spilled out of magazines and onto billboards along the road. The most humorous jingles promoted Burma-Shave, a shaving cream that could be applied without a brush. A series of low billboards, each bearing a verse, were spaced so that a motorist traveling 35 miles per hour could catch the message in about 18 seconds: HE PLAYED A SAX / HAD NO B.O. / BUT HIS WHISKERS SCRATCHED / SO SHE LET HIM GO. The last sign displayed the Burma-Shave logo. When Clinton and Allan Odell, the father and son behind Burma-Shave, ran out of rhymes, they sponsored an annual contest. They paid $100 for any jingle accepted. By the 1940s, more than 7,000 Burma-Shave ads studded American roadsides.

Billboards plastered with brand names, as well as signs for gas stations, hot dog stands, and flea markets, all competed for drivers' attention. Some roadside buildings were eye-catching creations in and of themselves. Motorists in southern California couldn't miss the green Toed Inn, for instance, shaped like a giant toad. In Kentucky, Frank Redford christened his auto court Wigwam Village. Motorists slept in steel tepees with showers, electricity, and a tribal touch: Navajo and Apache blankets. The lunchroom, housed in a 60-foot tepee, did not feature Native American cooking, however. Coca Cola cost 5 cents; Wigwam Breakfast No. 2, served anytime, consisted of country ham, eggs, toast, and coffee for 60 cents.

Not everyone delighted in garish signs and oddball architecture. In 1923, Elizabeth Lawton of Glens Falls, New York, founded the National Committee for the Restriction of Outdoor Advertising (later the National Council for the Protection of Roadside Beauty). She argued:

> The great stream of automobile traffic, increasing at a rate almost incredible, is trailing the commerce of the cities out along every country road, and the quiet beauty of our rural roads is fast giving way to the sordid ugliness of cheap commerce.

Allying with AAA and the Garden Club of America, Lawton enlisted about three million members. Beautification forces wrote slogans (A Sign Removed is a Scene Improved), organized design contests for roadside stands, and pushed companies to remove billboards.

But automobiles posed moral as well as visual dangers. The speed of change—and cars—in the 1920s alarmed older folks and dazzled the young. The youthful energy of the "Roaring Twenties" surfaced in music (jazz), architecture (the zigzag lines of art deco), and on the road. Cars enabled gun-toting gangsters to make getaways and young people to stray from home and family. They also offered romantic opportunities. The sight of "flappers" in short skirts necking with men in back seats disturbed conservative townspeople.

Cars symbolized youth, speed, and sex appeal in the 1920s.

Cars killed too. In 1930, 32,500 Americans died in auto-related accidents. In the era of Prohibition (1920–1933), the United States outlawed liquor; yet Philadelphia police arrested 494 drunken drivers in 1921 and 820 in 1925. The swiftness of the automobile revolution often left traffic unregulated. As a 1930 article in the *American Mercury* reported, 12 states imposed no speed limits, 28 didn't require driver's licenses, and South Carolina let 12-year-olds drive. So common were crashes that writers wove them into their novels—from F. Scott Fitzgerald's classic *The Great Gatsby* (1925) to one of the first Nancy Drew books, *The Mystery at Lilac Inn* (1930). A crossroads collision prompts one character in the mystery to wail, "Why will people insist upon speeding?" However, 16-year-old Nancy drives her "low-swung and smart" bright blue roadster sensibly as she solves the case.

Drivers not only injured each other but also regularly knocked down pedestrians, particularly kids. In the 1920s, AAA expanded its School Safety Patrol program. It outfitted children with white belts with a strap across the right shoulder and trained them as crossing guards. As part of its Save-A-Life campaign, AAA sponsored voluntary auto inspections, encouraging motorists to test brakes and headlights. Since teens were getting behind the wheel of the family car, in the 1930s AAA pioneered high school as well as adult driver's education.

"I'M GOIN' DOWN THAT ROAD FEELING BAD"
In the 1930s, the United States plunged into the Great Depression. Banks failed; wages and prices fell; farmers lost their land; homeless families huddled in shacks; laid-off laborers lined up at soup kitchens. By 1933, the unemployment rate had reached 24.9 percent. In Detroit, auto manufacturers cut back, retooled, or went out of business.

But, as the Lynds found when they returned to Muncie, even though many Americans couldn't afford to buy new cars, they continued to drive old ones. As comedian Will Rogers quipped, "We are the first nation in the history of the world to go to the poorhouse in an automobile."

Road construction continued—on a reduced scale—in the 1930s, mostly because it created jobs for the unemployed. Under President

Franklin Roosevelt's New Deal programs, the government spent about $4 billion building, improving, and repairing roads and streets. The Works Progress Administration, a New Deal agency, hired writers to produce guidebooks for motorists.

Roosevelt dreamed of building national superhighways; he admired the German autobahn, or expressway. With no stop signs or traffic lights, the autobahn allowed drivers to cruise at high speeds; cars entered and exited only at widely spaced interchanges. Although Roosevelt couldn't generate much support for high-speed, limited access expressways, smaller projects proved their worth. The Pennsylvania Turnpike, built as a government back-to-work project, followed an abandoned railroad route. Despite the $1.50 toll, 6,500 truckers and motorists a day drove on the turnpike during its first year. It cut travel time from Philadelphia to Pittsburgh almost in half.

Mobility gave people hope through the Great Depression. In his Pulitzer Prize-winning novel, *The Grapes of Wrath* (1939), John Steinbeck put a human face on the mass migration of "Okies" from Oklahoma and nearby states to California. Steinbeck's Joad family loses its farm due to

During the Great Depression, many poor farm families took to the road, looking for work, sometimes in old horse-drawn wagons. Yet automakers planned a bright future, with streamlined cars (opposite) and smooth superhighways.

the Depression and the Dust Bowl (the droughts and dust storms of the 1930s). They load their belongings into a rickety truck and head west on Route 66. Although the Joads meet endless difficulties, as long as they can move, they can continue searching for work and a better life. (The successful movie based on the book included footage of the real Route 66 and familiar scenes such as truck stops, gas station attendants in uniforms and bow ties, and sheep crossing the highway.)

In the very short lull between the Depression and World War II, Americans imagined "Building the World of Tomorrow," the theme of the much publicized 1939 World's Fair in New York. Visitors to the Highways and Horizons exhibit sponsored by General Motors rode gondolas over a model of the United States in 1960. This "Futurama" display included 500,000 tiny buildings and 50,000 teardrop-shaped cars and trucks that appeared to whip along superhighways. Pay no attention to today's wrecks and rutted roads, the exhibit suggested; tomorrow Americans will be zooming toward the brightest possible future.

CAUTION: DIVIDED HIGHWAY AHEAD

The automobile has not merely taken over the street, it has dissolved the living tissue of the city. Its appetite for space is absolutely insatiable; moved and parked, it devours urban land, leaving the buildings as mere islands of habitable space in a sea of dangers and ugly traffic.

—James Marston Fitch,
New York Times,
May 1, 1960

During World War II (1941–1945), automobile factories converted their assembly lines for the production of tanks, planes, and guns. Americans once again stopped buying new cars: none were being made. Citizens had to curtail their driving since the government rationed gas and tires (as well as sugar, coffee, and meat) in order to supply the military. Horse-drawn trucks reappeared, and workers carpooled or took the bus. Motorists even donated bumpers from their cars to the war effort—the metal was melted down and made into weapons. The home front lived by this motto: Use it up, wear it out, make it do, or do without.

When the war ended, Americans returned to "normal life" with enthusiasm. In 1949, 17-year-old Richard Arnoff climbed into the cab of one of his family's trucks and started hauling household goods all over the country. He felt like "a cowboy," making his own decisions, full of "the freedom and adventure of the road." Motoring south on Route 17 in the early 1950s, he crossed old wooden bridges. He slept underneath the truck or inside the cab wrapped in blankets. Like the wagoners of old, truckers stuck together and shared tips. Arnoff explains:

> It's almost a national club. . . .When I first started to drive, the big thing was you had to have a chain-drive wallet . . . a large leather wallet that had a chain, and the chain attached to your belt. You had to wear black engineer boots. That was a big thing. Your belt buckle always showed that you were with whatever company . . . or it had your name. . . . It was an identification situation really. Everybody wants to identify or become part of this national team feeling.

By 1946, the United States had paved half of its roads. But most were still narrow, dangerous, or simply inadequate for the volume of traffic. The trucking "team" and the usual pro-road forces pressed hard for wider, safer roads. They found an ally in President Dwight Eisenhower. As a general in World War II, Eisenhower had noted how efficiently the Germans mobilized troops and tanks via the autobahn. He

Above: World War II-era traffic jam. Opposite: three-story tire on route I-94 outside Detroit, 1990s

Workers pour concrete for a North Carolina interstate in the late 1950s.

backed a "National System of Interstate and Defense Highways." Initially designed to help city dwellers evacuate in case of nuclear attack, the system would prove to be more of a boon to commerce, tourism, and commuting.

The Interstate Highway Act of 1956 called for building 41,000 miles of new roads over several decades. While Washington set standards and bankrolled 90 percent of the project, state highway departments handled construction and maintenance. After much debate, Congress arrived at a means to pay for this ambitious project: a highway trust fund derived from federal taxes on fuels, tires, and inner tubes, as well as users' fees for heavy vehicles.

The United States had emerged from World War II as a superpower, and the whole country was thinking big. Earthmovers were soon leveling mountains. Forget Gunter's chain. Surveyors mapped terrain with "tellurometers," devices that used microwaves to measure distance. According to a glowing 1958 article in *Reader's Digest,* superhighways showed off American know-how:

Road building used to be something that college football play-
ers worked at during the summer vacation to build up their
muscles. But now they have to bring their professors along to
help with seismographs, hydraulic hoes, diamond saws, vibra-
tors, sheepsfoot rollers.

"SEE THE USA IN YOUR CHEVROLET"

In Detroit, the Big Three automakers (Ford, Chrysler, and General Motors) churned out cars at a record rate. Americans consumed with a
vengeance, as if collecting a reward after the sacrifices of World War II.
Many bought gas-guzzling sedans with flashy tail fins and extras such as
power steering and air conditioning. The average car cost about $1,200
in the 1950s, half a teacher's yearly salary. Big spenders could splurge on
a $14,000 Cadillac El Dorado Brougham—with a perfume bottle, lip-
stick case, tissue dispenser, and four gold drinking cups on the dashboard. Even that paled beside Elvis Presley's custom Caddy limousine.
The singer ordered a TV, record player, phone, bar, ice maker, and shoe
buffer installed in his car. His gold records plated the ceiling, white fur
carpeted the floor, and the exterior sparkled with a finish of crushed di-
amonds and fish scales.

By 1958, Americans were driving 67.4 million cars and trucks.
Roughly 12 million families owned *two*. Thanks to the GI Bill, which
made low-interest loans available to veterans, many families bought
houses. Wheels enabled them to leave the cities for the suburbs. In the
1950s, subdivision developments gobbled up about 3,000 acres of green
space per day. Cars shaped the suburban landscape. Builders attached
garages to houses as standard design. Drivers pulled into roadside strip
malls and, eventually, parking lots around shopping centers.

Drive-in businesses thrived: burger joints, dry cleaners, even funeral
homes. The Presbyterian Drive-In Church of Florida announced that it
provided "an extra spiritual dimension, brought on by the sun, pines
and birds." By 1956, there were 7,000 drive-in movie theaters. With a
speaker hooked onto a window, families watched musicals like *Guys and
Dolls* through the windshield.

For car buyers and automakers of the 1950s, bigger was better.

Movies both reflected and enlarged the American fascination with auto travel, as did the new medium of television. Hollywood scriptwriters could bank on the appeal of high-speed car chases. In plot after plot, the heady mix of speed and freedom at the wheel often overrode common sense, turning ordinary citizens into outlaws. Characters met on buses, escaped in cars, died in crashes. On the road, anything could happen. Route 66, an old two-lane highway, traversed the country from Chicago to southern California. In the TV series of the same name (1960–1964), actors Martin Milner and George Maharis cruised the highway in a Corvette, searching for adventure. In *The Long, Long Trailer* (1954), Lucille Ball and Desi Arnaz played road travel for laughs. The comic couple got nothing but trouble as they tried to maneuver their 40-foot mobile home into parking spaces, through busy city streets, and up narrow mountain roads.

Cars particularly fascinated young people. Getting a driver's license marked a passage to adulthood. Social life centered around cars. High school students hung out at drive-ins and diners and made out on dark "lovers' lanes." Rock-and-roll songs gave a beat to adolescent roaming. In 1935, GM had pioneered the instrument-panel radio, and by the 1950s passengers could hear their favorite AM stations by pushing a button. In "No Particular Place to Go" (1964), Chuck Berry describes the frustration of one young Romeo. He parks to smooch with his girl-friend—only to discover that he can't undo her seat belt. Even more than in the 1920s, roomy cars presented unmarried couples with the opportunity for sex.

The "generation gap" widened, in part because of mobility. Thirty-three million Americans moved in 1958, sometimes severing ties to communities and extended families. Rootless, restless kids occasionally drifted toward gangs and trouble. In a show of bravado, "hot-rodders" "drag raced" on straightaways or stole cars for brief "joy rides." Pop songs featured shattering glass and mourning lovers. Books such as *1,000,000 Delinquents* (1954) fed parents' fears of losing control of their kids. So did Hollywood movies. Marlon Brando starred as *The Wild One* (1954); James Dean as a *Rebel Without a Cause* (1955). Low-budget movies— *Lawless Streets, Dragstrip Girl*—dramatized the temptations and dangers of the road. After Dean died in a crash in 1956, fans paid 25 cents to sit behind the wheel of his death car.

Jack Kerouac's 1957 novel *On the Road*, based on a wild cross-country trip thumbing rides with a delinquent friend, climbed briefly onto the best-seller list. The book appalled critics, parents, and teachers but inspired a following among Kerouac's "beat generation." The next generation of "hippies" followed suit in the 1960s, touring the country in funky Volkswagen vans.

TOO MUCH OF A GOOD THING?

But the glorious automobile had a downside. In 1961, activist Jane Jacobs published an influential book linking interstate highways with the decline of the American city. Interstates frequently lured those who could afford cars deep into the suburbs. With the affluent people went tax money, stores, and businesses. Downtowns began to wither. Bus and streetcar lines shut down. Those who remained in urban areas cared about the decline, but they often lacked the means to stop it.

In rural areas, planners found cheap, vacant land for roads. New interstate highways unfurled on schedule. To link suburbs to city centers, however, planners had to run routes though existing urban neighborhoods. By law, the government could bulldoze houses by right of "eminent domain" (for the public good). Home owners were paid to relocate. But highway placement created ill will. Often the poorest neighborhoods, home to blacks and other minorities, were sacrificed for freeways. Roads

Movies like **Hot Rod Gang** *(1958) showed both cars and kids out of control.*

Downtown Baltimore. By the mid-1960s, many Americans were abandoning city life for more spacious suburbs.

divided cities, literally, into zones of rich and poor, black and white. Even economist John Kenneth Galbraith, who had celebrated American prosperity, began to criticize middle-class commuters "in their mauve and cerise, air-conditioned, power-steered and power-braked automobiles" passing through blighted cities without a twinge of compassion. As he wrote in *The Affluent Society* (1958), "Is this, indeed, American genius?"

Meanwhile, drivers discovered the woes of commuting. Tuning in to traffic reports over the radio, they learned from helicopters flying overhead when they could expect delays due to accidents or construction. According to the 1960 census, 65 percent of the working population drove to work.

Not only urban areas suffered when interstates went in. When Francis Turner, head of the Federal Highway Administration, planned a new interstate, he also crippled many of the small towns the road bypassed.

Freeways across Los Angeles, 1962

While they were enjoying the TV show, drivers abandoned the real Route 66 for the larger, faster superhighway. Mom-and-pop motels, gas stations, and restaurants along old routes went broke. Americans zooming along interstates saw more and more of the same national chains—Howard Johnson's, Kentucky Fried Chicken, McDonald's—businesses that could afford expensive land around the highway exits. As Holiday Inn promised, guests found "no surprises."

Americans soon longed for lost back roads. In 1962, John Steinbeck set out "in search of America" with his poodle, Charley, and wrote about their travels. For many years, CBS-TV evening news aired "On the Road" features by Charles Kuralt, who prowled around in a motor home filming quirky small-town happenings. In 1983, William Least Heat-Moon published *Blue Highways,* so titled because old highway maps marked main routes in red and lesser ones in blue. A sense of loss tinged his description of places like Nameless, Tennessee, and Scratch Ankle, Alabama.

POWER TO THE PEOPLE

By the 1960s, Americans could no longer ignore the problems caused by their beloved automobiles. In the tradition of 1920s crusader Elizabeth Lawton, Lady Bird Johnson, then first lady, led a beautification movement popular with garden clubs and civic groups. The effort persuaded Congress in 1964 to set aside money for planting flowers, removing billboards, and picking up litter along roadsides. Pulling heartstrings with public-service TV ads featuring Native Americans, the Keep America Beautiful campaign urged Americans to stop throwing paper cups and cigarette butts out car windows.

Citizens' groups worked to reroute proposed highways away from wetlands and historic neighborhoods. Planners could no longer build roads almost anywhere they pleased. Inner-city residents in Washington, D.C., chanted, "No white men's roads through black men's homes." One frustrated federal official complained in 1964, "The most serious obstacles in our roadbuilding program are not money, nor engineering problems, nor cruel terrain—but PEOPLE."

Meanwhile, air pollution—smog—was fouling American cities. Factory smokestacks spewed some of the filth. But car exhaust and evaporating gasoline contributed greatly to the problem. Repeated smog scares helped mobilize the growing environmental movement (in 1953, 240 people with heart and lung ailments died when weather conditions trapped a layer of polluted air over New York City). Young people drew the nation's attention to the issue with humor and energy. They printed T-shirts with slogans like "I shot an arrow in the air—and it stuck." In 1968, the Broadway cast of *Hair* sang about carbon monoxide—a toxic gas in car exhaust. On the first Earth Day, in 1970, students bashed cars as a symbolic protest.

Although businesses often opposed environmental regulation, the price of pollution—$11 billion in property damage (corrosion of buildings, for example) from smog alone in 1966—convinced lawmakers to act. California led the nation in requiring the first antipollution devices on cars in the 1960s. In 1970 Congress passed the Clean Air Act, which in part ordered exhaust controls on all vehicles.

The United States burned the lion's share of the world's fossil fuels—oil, gas, and coal. In the 1970s, Arab producers cut oil supplies to the United States. The sudden shortage forced gas prices to rise and drivers to line up at the pumps. The "energy crisis" shocked car owners. Perhaps for the first time, people realized that fuel supplies weren't going to last forever.

Concerned citizens pushed for funds to revive mass transit. Subway lines, buses, and streetcars—many of which had been shut down during the car-buying boom of the 1950s—could carry dozens of commuters using not much more fuel than it took to transport just a few people by automobile. Although people weren't willing to give up driving, many switched from roomy American-made sedans to smaller, cheaper, imported cars that used less gas (and fit into smaller parking spaces).

Car owners were learning that they couldn't always trust government and business to look out for their best interests. They had to be vigilant consumers. As a young lawyer, Ralph Nader took on the Big Three and made that point clear. Investigating the tendency of GM Corvairs to flip

Ralph Nader

over, Nader found that automakers put sales before safety. Although the Big Three knew that seat belts saved lives, they didn't alert customers. In fact, the car companies made seat belts an option that cost extra. They also sold cars too big for their tires or with faulty brakes. In 1965, 49,000 Americans died in 13 million auto accidents. That year, Nader attacked the American auto industry's claims of superior engineering in *Unsafe at Any Speed*. The book stirred the public and spurred Congress to pass the Traffic and Motor Vehicle Safety Act a year later, which required seat belts in all cars, as well as other safety features. Eventually, states also required people to *buckle* the seat belts. By the 1990s, automakers were installing air bags, cushioning devices that inflate during accidents, as standard features.

Candy Lightner started another safety movement—this one directed at drivers. In 1980, a drunk driver killed Lightner's 13-year-old daughter, Cari. Lightner tracked the man down—out on bail from a previous accident. Angry that the courts treated drunk drivers so leniently, Lightner organized Mothers Against Drunk Driving (MADD). Among their many activities, MADD members lobby for stricter penalties for drunk drivers and place crosses and flowers on roadsides to mark the sites of fatal crashes.

AN I-WAY FOR THE TWENTY-FIRST CENTURY

Safety, beautification, environmentalism, community activism—all these concerns shape road travel at the end of the 20th century. So, too, does the budget crunch. Already in debt, with many worthy programs to support, state and federal government cannot fund much new road construction. Nor can government keep every mile of America's vast network of roads, bridges, and tunnels in tip-top shape. While listening closely to citizen input, highway officials must juggle dollars and opinions.

California transportation engineer Art Salazar says that many people

Trucks haul raw material and finished products to and from factories, farms, stores, and warehouses.

plead "nimby"—*not in my b*ackyard—at the proposal of a new road. But others welcome roads as a way to bring businesses, jobs, commuters, and tourism to their communities. Before Salazar starts designing a road, he has to study its potential impact:

> Before you decide to connect two points, you need to see what's out there. Are there areas you need to avoid? You can't build a road through an area in which they're already planning low-income housing.... Is there a mountain here? It's too expensive to tunnel through a mountain, so can you build around it? There's a swamp over here; there's a park here. If you get to choose between going through a park or going through a housing project, which would you choose? What would be the basis of your decision?... Once you've got all those things determined, the actual building of the road is the easy part.

According to David Malsch, a 29-year veteran of the Washington State Department of Transportation (DOT), such problems present opportunities for engineers. When building a section of I-90 into Seattle, for instance, planners faced numerous setbacks. A court order, rising land costs, community protests, and environmental issues delayed the project for years. But Malsch thinks the process resulted in a better road. It includes a bridge that floats on concrete pontoons and a tunnel with three levels: one for commuter trains and car pools, one for regular traffic, and one for pedestrians and bicyclists.

Now that the interstate building program is "sunsetting," the emphasis of many highway departments has shifted toward "preservation of existing structures and safety enhancements," says Malsch. Maintenance includes patching holes, removing rocks, even closing the road temporarily and setting off avalanches before snow slides onto unsuspecting motorists. "If we were to stop maintenance," says Malsch, "inside of two or three years we wouldn't be able to travel from one side of the state to the other."

The New York State Thruway Authority concentrates on safety and law enforcement as well as upkeep. Tolls pay for 325 troopers who patrol just the thruway. "You have to be a kind of jack-of-all-trades," says state police sergeant Tom Ferritto. Criminals—particularly drug smugglers—depend on good roads to transport contraband. So troopers, in radio contact with watchful toll collectors, keep an eye out for suspicious activity. Mostly, though, troopers respond to emergencies—flat tires, collisions, the occasional pregnant woman in labor. In 1994, a speeding tractor-trailer overturned, releasing about 1.5 million agitated honeybees. Besides sending the driver to the hospital (along with a good Samaritan who got badly stung) state police stopped traffic and consulted bee experts. They called in fire trucks to spray sugar water. When that failed to pacify the bees, the trucks sprayed pesticides. In the meantime, they reopened the road and put out an advisory for motorists to roll up their windows.

Troopers also act as a public conscience. They arrest drunk drivers, stop parents who have failed to strap their children in car seats, weigh trucks to make sure they're not carrying more than 18,000 pounds per axle, and ticket speeders. Sergeant Ferritto estimates that over 7½ years he has issued about 25,000 speeding tickets. Once he clocked a Jaguar flying down the thruway at 124 miles per hour.

As the United States heads into the 21st century, its past travels with it. Old roads and new roads coexist. From New York City to Albany, for instance, drivers can choose routes from among three eras. Route 9, on the east bank of the Hudson River, probably began as an Indian footpath. It's also known as the Albany Post Road, from the days when stagecoaches used it to carry mail. Farther east lies the Taconic Parkway, a winding, leafy route that motorists in the 1920s used to escape the city for a Sunday drive. West of the river runs the flat, smooth thruway, the epitome of late 20th-century efficiency and speed.

The information superhighway—the developing worldwide network (Internet) of computers—will probably not put other roads out of business. In fact, the New York State Thruway has teamed up with industry to lay fiber-optic cable for the Internet along the road's right-of-way. The Internet is changing road travel, though. More people are working at home, communicating with their offices via computer. Studies suggest this trend will mean less rush-hour traffic.

Richard Arnoff predicts more automation in the trucking business. Modern tractor-trailers include all the conveniences of a mobile home, and many have onboard computers that enable truckers to compare mileage on different routes, calculate rates for freight, and check in with home offices. Car drivers conduct business on the road, too, chattering on cellular phones and sending faxes with laptop computers.

But no electronic connection is going to be able to move living room furniture, pick up groceries, or transport a family to the Grand Canyon. As essayist E. B. White once observed, "Everything in life is somewhere else, and you get there in a car."

SELECTED BIBLIOGRAPHY

Barnes, Demas. *From the Atlantic to the Pacific, overland.* 1866. Reprint. New York: Arno Press, 1973.

Earle, Alice Morse. *Colonial Days in Old New York.* 1896. Reprint. Port Washington, N.Y.: N.p. 1962.

Finch, Christopher. *Highways to Heaven: The AUTO Biography of America.* New York: HarperCollins, 1992.

Flink, James J. *The Car Culture.* Cambridge, Mass.: MIT Press, 1975.

Goddard, Stephen B. *Getting There: The Epic Struggle between Road and Rail in the American Century.* New York: Basic Books, 1994.

Gordon, Lois and Alan. *American Chronicle: Six Decades in American Life, 1920–1980.* New York: Atheneum, 1987.

Holmes, Oliver W., and Peter T. Rohrbach. *Stagecoach East: Stagecoach Days in the East from the Colonial Period to the Civil War.* Washington: Smithsonian Institution Press, 1983.

Jakle, John A. *The American Small Town: Twentieth-Century Place Images.* Hamden, Conn.: Archon Books, 1982.

Jennings, Jan, ed. *Roadside America: The Automobile in Design and Culture.* Ames: Iowa State University Press, 1990.

Keeshin, John Lewis. *No Fears, Hidden Tears: A Memoir of Fourscore Years.* Chicago: Castle-Pierce Press, 1983.

McLuhan, T. C. *Dream Tracks: The Railroad and the American Indian, 1890–1930.* New York: Harry N. Abrams, Inc., 1985.

Miller, Douglas and Marion Nowak. *The Fifties: The Way We Really Were.* Garden City, N.Y.: Doubleday & Company, Inc., 1977.

Mowry, George. *The Twenties: Fords, Flappers and Fanatics.* Englewood Cliffs, N.J.: Prentice-Hall, Inc., 1963.

Partridge, Bellamy. *Fill 'Er Up! The Story of Fifty Years of Motoring.* New York: McGraw-Hill Book Company, Inc. 1952.

Rae, John B. *The Road and the Car in American Life.* Cambridge, Mass.: MIT Press, 1971.

Ramsey, Alice Huyler. *Veil, Duster, and Tire Iron.* Covina, Calif.: Castle Press, 1961.

Rodes, Barbara and Rice Odell, eds. *A Dictionary of Environmental Quotations.* New York: Simon & Schuster, 1992.

Schlissel, Lillian. *Women's Diaries of the Westward Journey.* New York: Schocken Books, 1982.

Sears, Stephen. *Hometown U.S.A.* New York: American Heritage Publishing Co., Inc., 1975.

Steinbeck, John. *Travels with Charley: In Search of America.* New York: Viking Press, 1962.

Stewart, George. *U.S. 40: Cross Section of the United States of America.* Cambridge, Mass.: Riverside Press, 1953.

Stilgoe, John R. *Common Landscapes of America, 1580 to 1845.* New Haven, Conn.: Yale University Press, 1982.

Tunis, Edwin. *Frontier Living.* New York: World Publishing Company, 1961.

Wallace, Paul. *Indian Paths of Pennsylvania.* Harrisburg: Pennsylvania Historical and Museum Commission, 1987.

Works Progress Administration. *U.S. One: Maine to Florida.* 1938. Reprint. New York: Modern Age Books, Inc., 1972.

Yoder, Paton. *Taverns and Travelers: Inns of the Early Midwest.* Bloomington: Indiana University Press, 1969.

INDEX

ACKNOWLEDGMENTS

Photographs and illustrations used with permission of Archive Photos: pp. 2, 3, 72; Archive/American Stock: pp. 42, 72; Archive/Enell: p. 54; Archive/Levick: p. 52; Archive/Price: p. 67; Virginia State Library and Archives: pp. 6, 20; © Ed Kashi: p. 7; Museum of New Mexico: pp. 9 (46535), 28 (76990), 29 (Jesse L. Nusbaum/61818), 31 (139983), 38 top (Dana B. Chase/2267), 38 bottom (7741), 57 (46940), 59 (46923); Library of Congress: pp. 12, 13, 18, 25, 35, 46, 60, 88; Historic Urban Plans, Ithaca, New York: p. 14; Colorado Historical Society: p. 16; Union Station Museum, Ogden, Utah: p. 27; Colorado Springs Pioneers Museum, Starsmore Center for Local History: p. 32; State Historical Society of Wisconsin: p. 34 [Whi(V2)CF547]; American Automobile Manufacturers Association: pp. 36, 40, 43, 62, 69, 70; © American Automobile Association: pp. 41, 48; Detroit Public Library, National Automotive History Collection: pp. 45, 49; Ford Motor Company: p. 47; Tennessee State Library and Archives: p. 50; National Archives: pp. 55, 66, 76; Michelin North America: p. 68; Hollywood Book and Poster: p. 74; Independent Picture Service: p. 75; UPI/Bettmann: p. 79; Freightliner Corporation: p. 80; © Charlene Faris: p. 83.

Front cover: Darren Erickson
Back cover: Library of Congress